Cooking SCHOOL

American Food

SARA GILBERT

CREATIVE EDUCATION & CREATIVE PAPERBACKS

Published by Creative Education and Creative Paperbacks
P.O. Box 227, Mankato, Minnesota 56002 • Creative Education
and Creative Paperbacks are imprints of The Creative Company
www.thecreativecompany.us

Design and production by Christine Vanderbeek
Printed in the United States of America

Photographs by Corbis (Bettmann, William Brady/Retna Ltd.),
iStockphoto (EasyBuy4u, IvonneW, mphillips007, naelnabil),
Shutterstock (area381, elsyl, EM Arts, Rob Hainer, HLPhoto, Oliver
Hoffmann, Vitaly Korovin, berna namoglu, NEGOVURA, KIM
NGUYEN, nioloxs, Pinkyone, pogonici, Sailorr, Shaiith, Danny
Smythe, SOMMAI, Evlakhov Valeriy, VolkOFF-ZS-BP, Yganko),
Christine Vanderbeek

Library of Congress Cataloging-in-Publication Data
Gilbert, Sara. • American food / by Sara Gilbert. • p. cm. —
(Cooking school) • Summary: An elementary introduction to
the relationship between cooking and American culture, the
effect of local agriculture on the diets of different regions,
common tools such as grills, and recipe
instructions. • Includes biblio-
graphical references and
index. • ISBN 978-1-60818-
500-9 (hardcover) • ISBN
978-1-62832-094-7 (pbk)
1. Cooking, American—
Juvenile literature. 2. Food—
United States—Juvenile
literature. I. Title.
TX715.G473 2015
641.5973—dc23
2014002295

CCSS: RI.1.1, 2, 3, 5, 6, 7;
RI.2.1, 2, 3, 5, 6, 7; RI.3.1, 3,
5, 7; RF.1.1; RF.2.3, 4; RF.3.3

First Edition
9 8 7 6 5 4 3 2 1

Table of Contents

Delicious Foods

People cook everywhere. They cook big meals and small snacks. It's fun to make *nutritious* food that tastes good. In the United States, cooks make many different kinds of foods from coast to coast.

Turkey is the star of a typical American Thanksgiving meal.

Coming to America

The U.S. includes people who came from many different countries. They brought their *recipes* with them. They made up new recipes in America, too.

As Americans moved west in the 1800s, they hunted for food.

Taste of the U.S.

People in the Northeast cook with seafood such as lobsters and clams. They are known for making clam *chowder*.

Seafood can be eaten whole (opposite) or as part of other dishes.

In the Midwest, farmers grow vegetables such as corn and grains such as oats and wheat. Apples grow there, too. Apple pie is a favorite dessert.

Fried chicken is popular in the South. Sometimes people eat it with mashed potatoes and cornbread or biscuits.

People from Scotland and Africa brought fried chicken to the U.S.

Western *ranches* raise cattle for steaks and hamburgers. Farmers grow potatoes in Idaho, lettuce in California, and cherries in Washington.

Grilling Out

Many Americans have a grill outside. Some grills use gas to cook food. Others use charcoal fires.

Mini apple pies

are a yummy dessert for one person to eat!

INGREDIENTS

6 tablespoons flour

¾ cup sugar

1½ teaspoons ground cinnamon

2 large Granny Smith apples

1 prepared piecrust

butter

ice cream for serving

DIRECTIONS

1. With an adult's help, preheat oven to 400 °F.

2. Mix 6 tablespoons flour, ¾ cup sugar, and 1½ teaspoons ground cinnamon in a large bowl.

3. Peel and cut 2 large Granny Smith apples into small chunks. Stir into the flour mixture.

4. Unroll a prepared piecrust. Using a round cookie cutter or small glass, cut 12 circles out of the crust. Place one circle in each cup of a muffin pan. Use smaller cookie cutters to cut shapes from the remaining crust.

5. Spoon some of the apple mixture into each muffin cup. Place a small piece of butter on top of the apples, then top with the extra crust cutouts.

6. Bake 18 to 22 minutes. Serve warm, with ice cream!

Cornbread

is a delicious side dish or snack.

INGREDIENTS

2 tablespoons melted butter

1¼ cups flour

¾ cup cornmeal

½ cup sugar

2 teaspoons baking powder

½ teaspoon salt

1 cup milk

¼ cup oil

1 egg

butter and honey for serving

DIRECTIONS

1. With an adult's help, preheat oven to 400 °F. Put 2 tablespoons melted butter in a square pan.

2. Mix together 1¼ cups flour, ¾ cup cornmeal, ½ cup sugar, 2 teaspoons baking powder, and ½ teaspoon salt. Add 1 cup milk, ¼ cup oil, and 1 egg, and stir.

3. Pour batter into pan with melted butter and bake for 20 minutes. Poke a toothpick into the center. When it comes out clean, the cornbread is done!

4. Serve warm with butter and honey.

Cheeseburgers

on the grill are a family favorite all over the U.S.

INGREDIENTS

ground beef

cheese slices

fresh buns

lettuce

tomatoes

pickles

DIRECTIONS

1. Make four round patties of ground beef. Ask an adult to help you grill them.

2. When the burgers are almost cooked, top with a slice of cheese.

3. Serve on fresh buns with lettuce, tomatoes, and pickles. Enjoy!

Glossary

chowder a rich soup often using fish with potatoes and onions

nutritious healthy and good for you

ranches large farms where animals are raised

recipes sets of instructions for making a certain dish, including a list of ingredients

Read More

Blaxland, Wendy. *I Can Cook! American Food.* Mankato, Minn.: Smart Apple Media, 2011.

Graimes, Nicola. *Kids' Fun and Healthy Cookbook.* London: DK Children, 2007.

Low, Jennifer. *Kitchen for Kids.* New York: Whitecap Books, 2010.

Websites

http://www.pbs.org/food/theme/cooking-with-kids/
Find easy recipes to try by yourself or with an adult's assistance.

http://www.foodnetwork.com/cooking-with-kids/package/index.html
Learn to cook with celebrity chefs on the website of television's Food Network.

Note: Every effort has been made to ensure that the websites listed above are suitable for children, that they have educational value, and that they contain no inappropriate material. However, because of the nature of the Internet, it is impossible to guarantee that these sites will remain active indefinitely or that their contents will not be altered.

Index